JONATHAN SWIFT

JONATHAN SWIFT

Selected Poems

Edited with an introduction by C. H. Sisson

FyfieldBooks

First published in 1977
First published in this joint edition in 1990 by
Carcanet Press Limited
208–212 Corn Exchange Buildings
Manchester M4 3BQ
and
The Blackstaff Press Limited
3 Galway Park, Dundonald
Belfast BT16 0AN

ISBN 0-85635-135-0 Carcanet
ISBN 0-85640-442-X Blackstaff

The publishers acknowledge financial assistance
from the Arts Council of Great Britain.

Printed in England by SRP Ltd, Exeter

CONTENTS

INTRODUCTION

THERE IS nothing moth-eaten about the figure of Jonathan Swift. One of the greatest writers in the English language, and living in a time which seems formal and hierarchic in comparison with our own, he speaks across two hundred and fifty years with freshness and directness, and nowhere more so than in the best of his poems.

It is not that Swift was a simple character. Far from it. The complexity of his attitudes, both personal and political, is such that he remains an enigma in spite of generations of biographers and critics. Yet his complexity and his directness are allied. Lesser figures can think abstruse thoughts, or cultivate their personal feelings, while ignoring most of what goes on in the world around them. Swift took account of the doings and sayings of great and small, which is not at all the same thing as being at the mercy of prevailing opinion —he was certainly not that. He had a marvellous ear for talk and delighted in popular eccentricities of speech.

The greatness of Swift is rather in his prose than in his poetry. There are some twenty volumes of prose writings, if one includes the letters. Most of it is of an occasional character, arising out of the events of the day, in which he took a passionate and sometimes jealous interest. He had had enough experience of affairs not to over-value those who were in charge of the nation's fortunes. He could be peremptory both to men in government and to people who pretended to know something about these things, and in fact knew nothing. His verse is *all* occasional. Some few poems relate to the great affairs of the day, which take so much place in his prose; much of it is the product of small social encounters and domestic events, or is written merely for the amusement of his friends and himself. He is a social and sociable poet, not one given to solitary musings. Yet his work is generally remote in tone from what is ordinarily understood by *vers de société*, for even in the lightest productions one feels something of the presence of a formidable hand, which can twitch aside the dressings of propriety in a moment, and show the pitiful figures underneath without any protection from cant or pretence. The poems fill more than six hundred and fifty large pages in the complete Oxford edition. What is here offered to the reader is a sample which illustrates the liveliness, humour and plain-speaking of this part of the author's works.

There is much more which anyone bitten by the tone of Swift's writing will want, in the end, to become acquainted with. Indeed, with a writer of Swift's genius, there is always something of the author at the tip of his pen. What sort of man was Swift? Here, one can give only a few indications. He was born in Dublin, but he attached more importance to the fact that he came of an old Yorkshire family, and was careful to say that one of his forebears who was made 'an Irish peer' by James I or Charles I 'was never in that country'. His father, who died before Swift was born, had some employment in Dublin. His mother, who was of a Leicestershire family, went back to England while he was still a child, and his upbringing was left in the hands of an uncle, who sent him to Kilkenny School and to Trinity College, Dublin.

It is important to remember how far Swift's roots were in the seventeenth century. The date of his birth was 1667—only seven years after the Restoration. His family connections were markedly Anglican and Royalist, and his uncle gave great offence by marrying, as one of his four successive wives, a connection of one of the regicides. These radical attitudes are of immense importance in Swift's work, though they can easily be missed by the casual reader of *Gulliver* and the more personal of the poems. He was a Church and State man after the first generation of Tories, a savage and realistic critic, when he saw the necessity, of ministers and other public men. He spoke for liberty, as his epitaph says.

At Trinity College Swift did not distinguish himself. He speaks of his own dullness and insufficiency, but the joke is against the college. He was of a nature to keep a certain distance between himself and the authorities. He did not care excessively for the scheduled courses, and preferred his own readings in history and poetry. There is no reason to suppose that he would have been content, at this age, at Oxford or Cambridge. The significant thing is that his formative years were spent among the stresses of Ireland.

Swift's career at Trinity College came to an end when the troubles broke out at the end of James II's reign. There is no reason to suppose that James had any special kindness for the native Irish, but their politics and his found a common meeting ground in the Roman Catholic interest. A flood of Irishry flowed over the pale, in the form of Tyrconnel's troops, who were quartered all over Dublin. Swift went to his mother in Leicestershire and afterwards took up residence at Moor Park, near Farnham in Surrey, with Sir William Temple.

It was a singular piece of good fortune which put Swift to this finishing-school. Temple was an accomplished man of affairs, and had some literary pretensions. He had been to school in Penshurst, the home of the Sidneys, and then to Emmanuel College, Cambridge, where he had been under the care of the Platonist Cudworth, an exponent of a kind of Christian rationalism. During the reign of Charles II Temple had been employed in Dutch affairs, and in this way had grown to be on familiar terms with the Prince of Orange, when the latter was only nineteen. It was this accident which gave Swift his earliest acquaintance with the court; Temple gave him opportunity, while he was still a young man, of trying—unsuccessfully—to give advice to William III. Temple had a good deal of vanity, and some tepid virtue. Swift in the end disappointed him by turning out to be, in reality, very much the man Temple was, in his own eyes. 'I knew very well', Temple says, 'the arts of a court are, to talk the present language, to serve the present turn, and to follow the present humour of the prince, whatever it is: of all these I found myself so incapable, that I could not talk a language I did not mean, nor serve a turn I did not like, nor follow any man's humour, wholly against my own.' That describes, precisely, the sort of awkward customer Swift became. Worse still, Swift turned out to have the originality and independence of a great writer, which must have been dispiriting for the *littérateur* in Temple.

Swift as a young man was anxious to get on in the world, and he came to be resentful that Temple did not, as he thought, do enough for him, as he had been ungrateful to his uncle for giving him 'the education of a dog'. The Church hardly counts, in these days, as one of the roads to advancement, but in those times it did and Swift's thoughts about an ecclesiastical career cannot have been free from worldliness. Yet there is very strong evidence that he was scrupulous about such matters. He had a profound respect, one might say reverence, for the saintly Sancroft, the archbishop of Canterbury who had been ejected because he could not take the oath of allegiance to William while James was still alive. Swift himself would not enter Holy Orders until he had the offer of lay employment, which he turned down, so that it could not be said that he became a priest for the sake of a living. He was none the less, like many clerics of earlier times, very much a man of the world. He reached his early forties without any employment which measured up to his wishes. Then, towards the end of 1710, came the meeting with Harley, and for three years he lived close to the centre of the political business of the day. He became the close collaborator of Harley, the leader of the Tory administration, and of St John (Bolingbroke). These brief years were, probably, the only ones of his life when he felt he had the career for which his talents fitted him. Yet there was an element of illusion about those exciting years. Probably Swift was not so much in Harley's confidence as he thought he was. In any case, when we look back on Swift we can see that the main importance of this period of his life was that it gave the final polish to his knowledge of the world, and so the final touch of authority to those later writings in which, from the deanery in Dublin to which he was in effect banished, he arraigned the Whig masters who had by then taken control of the eighteenth century.

Although this episode of public life was crucial in Swift's development, and public affairs continued to occupy his attention, in one form or another, for many years, it is no less important for the reader of the poems to know something of his private existence. There is the relationship with Stella, to whom the *Journal* of 1710-13 was addressed and whom he had met for the first time at Moor Park, when she was only seven years old. There were the relations with Vanessa, which were the subject of his longest poem, *Cadenus and Vanessa*, a work of great biographical interest, which considerations of space have excluded from this volume. Swift's relations with women are a subject of which much had been made, usually to Swift's disadvantage. A suspicion of sexual coldness, in this powerful character, has naturally made him an object of moral disapproval, in the twentieth century. Swift certainly enjoyed the company of women, and with men and women alike he had an undoubted capacity for friendship, openness, and plain-speaking. If

10

he looked after his pence rather carefully, he was generous to the needy. Always on his dignity with great men, so that anyone who gave himself airs with him did so at his peril, he was able to keep his end up also with the roughest labourers. More than most, in his age or in any other, he had the ability to be on familiar terms with people from the top to the bottom of the social scale.

Swift did not want to go back to Ireland, and regarded the deanery of St Patrick's as no great catch, as indeed it was not, for a man with his abilities and, for a time, political advantages. Yet it was the disappointment of his hopes which made him the great figure he became, in the end, as the spokesman of the population of Ireland. It was this which gave him the right to that epitaph which said he had exerted himself to the utmost for liberty—a term which he understood in a Roman and an old English sense. He would have been surprised at some more recent Irish usages.

When Swift first started to write, it was in verse. He certainly did not know what he was doing, even in the measure in which that is vouchsafed to poets. In a letter of 3 May 1692, to his cousin Thomas Swift, he describes the process as it appeared to him. 'Nor does it enter my head', he says, 'to make anything of a sudden except by great chance. I esteem the time of studying Poetry to be 2 hours in a morning, and that only when the humour sits, which I esteem for the flower of the whole day.' Keats at one time sat down to work in this way, but with a difference. With Swift the process was conscious and laborious; this was not poetry which came 'as easily as the leaves of a tree'. He tells us that he seldom wrote 'above 2 Stanzas in a week', and he altered them 'a hundred times, and yet', he adds, 'I do not believe myself to be a laborious dry writer.' He was evidently feeling his way, knowing or suspecting that he had great powers, but unable yet to use them. Seeing the results of these lucubrations, one does not readily think of the writer's processes as being much akin to those of a young man of our own day. Yet they were not much different. Swift was under the influence, not of the best models available to him, but of Abraham Cowley at his most inflated. It was not *The Mistress*, with its weak pastiche of more vigorous Metaphysical poetry, which interested Swift at this time, but the

Pindarique Odes, with their pompous preciosity and their array of notes. Such matter was calculated to fascinate a young man with an aptitude for verbal forms, and it attracted Swift as young poets have always been attracted by a series of fashions which appear silly enough to everyone at a later date. The art of the Pindaric, as practised by Cowley, consisted in the irregular number of syllables in the lines, producing, it may be supposed, the effect of surprise, if not astonishment, and a certain wilful lunacy in the sequence of thoughts.

The first survivor, among Swift's inventions in this kind, is probably the 'Ode to the King on his Irish Expedition'. The Pindaric lunacy is caught to perfection:

> And now I in the Spirit see
> (The Spirit of Exalted Poetry)
> I see the *Fatal Fight* begin;
> And, lo! where a Destroying Angel stands,
> (By all but Heaven and Me unseen)

—and so on. The Angel is uncomplimentary to the Irish. He says that it is no use their island boasting that there are no snakes (or words to that effect)

> *When Man himself's* the Vermin *of Her Earth*
> *When* Treason *there in* Person *seems to stand,*
> *And* Rebel *is the* growth *and* manufacture *of the Land.*

One has no difficulty in seeing Swift in those lines. The second ode was 'To the Athenian Society'. Swift must have been a considerable innocent when, at the age of twenty-four or so, he wrote that poem. He takes leave of his senses in a truly Pindaric way:

> Pardon Ye great Unknown, and far-exalted Men,
> The wild excursions of a youthful pen;
> Forgive a young and (almost) *Virgin-Muse*.

The great Unknown, including Dunton the bookseller, readily forgave Swift, for they printed not only his poem but the letter of submission that went with it, which had the merit of being dated from Moor Park, and so of advertising the author's—and the Society's—relations with Temple.

Leslie Stephen has an excellent phrase about Swift's early poems. He speaks of them as having 'one merit common to all his writing—

12

the merit of a thorough, sometimes an appalling, sincerity'. Even the absurd conventions of his medium could not obscure this congenital truthfulness, any more than the conventions of an allegedly 'natural' style now prevent the ordinary versifier from shrouding himself in lies. 'I take it to be part of the Honesty of Poets', Swift wrote in that letter to his cousin which has already been quoted, 'that they cannot write well except they think the subject deserves it.'

The early poem which best illustrates what Swift was thinking, at this time, is the 'Ode to Dr William Sancroft', whose life was governed by principles clean contrary to those of the accommodating man of affairs. There is no doubt of the specifically theological turn of Swift's mind in this poem. In an image of weather-cocks, he sets the mutations of the state over against the fixed direction of the Church. He sees Sancroft as acting on the pattern of Christ himself, bearing 'with heavenly peace of mind' 'the giddy turns of pop'lar rage'. This is woven inextricably with a Caroline royalism. He speaks of 'governments too easy', and laments

> Evils which a too gentle king,
> Too flourishing a spring,
> And too warm summers bring.

He is, of course, thinking of Charles I.

None of these early poems is included in this selection; they are interesting for the light they throw on Swift's development rather than for themselves. The first poem given here dates from 1699, when Swift was thirty-two and already a master of versification. 'Mrs Harris's Petition' exhibits the unequalled gift he had for catching the tone and rhythm of ordinary speech—the ordinary speech of uneducated people—and carrying it into a scheme of verse and rhyme. One has to go back to the sixteenth century, to that extraordinary little book the *Proverbs* of John Heywood (1562) for anything comparable:

> Ah, sir (said my friend), when men will needs marry,
> I see now, how wisdom and haste may vary:
> Namely, where they wed for love altogether.
> I would for no good, but I had come hither.
> Sweet beauty with sour beggary! nay, I am gone
> To the wealthy withered widow, by St John!

This sort of thing goes on, with Heywood, for something like a hundred pages. Swift's performance is briefer, but the edge of wit is sharper. There are other examples of this style, which involves a direct transference of common speech into verse (e.g. 'Mary the Cook-maid's Letter', p. 27), but the relationship with the popular roots of language is generally less direct. Yet there is always a link with the spoken word, though it is often—and why not?—with the language of the polite and well-educated; not that politeness, with Swift, ever takes us out of reach of the devastating thrust of his satire. There is no mincing matters for him. His stomach was a strong one.

It is less important than it once was to defend Swift's verse from the charge of being *unpoetic*. Throughout the nineteenth century, and well into the twentieth, it was felt that something was missing, in such directness. Certainly there is not a trace of the aura of romanticism. Even in the eighteenth century some uneasiness was felt. Johnson, as usual, is the best guide:

> In the poetical works of Dr Swift there is not much upon which the critic can exercise his powers. They are often humorous, almost always light, and have the qualities which recommend such compositions—easiness and gaiety. They are, for the most part, what their author intended. The diction is correct, the numbers are smooth, and the rhymes exact. There seldom occurs a hard-laboured expression or a redundant epithet; all his verses exemplify his own definition of a good style, they consist of *proper words in proper order*.

Beside the high-flown praise sometimes accorded to poets, that is not much; but for this kind of writing, it is everything.

The twentieth century, emerging from a long bout of romanticism, has looked at Swift differently. It was not into a new classicism that the century emerged, in spite of some brave gestures in the earlier decades. It was into a world obsessed, more than any classic balance could tolerate, by sex and personality. So, even when so astringent a writer as Edgell Rickword praised Swift's poems—and he was one of the first to make out a critical case for them—it was, by reaction, to pick out for especially favourable mention the qualities at the opposite pole from the aspirations of romanticism.

14

Rickword presents Swift as the exemplar of 'the poetry of negative emotions, of those arising from disgust with the object'. 'The Lady's Dressing-Room' is the type of this style of writing. For Rickword, of course, as for most of his contemporaries, it was 'a commonplace' that 'Swift was morbid'. So was D. H. Lawrence, and it is a mark of our distance from anything like classicism that his particular morbidities are so enthusiastically preferred. Goldsmith—as Herbert Read pointed out in an excellent essay on Swift—'said that Swift was the first poet who dared to describe nature as it is with all its deformities, and to give exact expression to a turn of thought alike dry, sarcastic, and severe'. As a characterisation of the peculiar merits of the poetical works of Swift, that sentence could hardly be bettered.

To Their Excellencies the Lords Justices of Ireland
THE HUMBLE PETITION OF FRANCES HARRIS,
Who must starve, and die a maid if it miscarries

Humbly Showeth
That I went to warm my self in Lady Betty's chamber, because
        I was cold,
And I had in a purse, seven pound, four shillings and six pence,
        besides farthings, in money, and gold;
So because I had been buying things for my lady last night,
I was resolved to tell my money, to see if it was right:
Now you must know, because my trunk has a very bad lock,
Therefore all the money, I have, which, God knows, is a very small
        stock,
I keep in a pocket tied about my middle, next my smock.
So when I went to put up my purse, as God would have it, my
        smock was unript,
And, instead of putting it into my pocket, down it slipt:
Then the bell rung, and I went down to put my lady to bed,
And, God knows, I thought my money was as safe as my maidenhead.
So when I came up again, I found my pocket feel very light,
But when I search'd, and miss'd my Purse, Lord! I thought I should
        have sunk outright:
Lord! Madam, says Mary, how d'ye do? Indeed, said I, never worse;
But pray, Mary, can you tell what I have done with my purse!
Lord help me, said Mary, I never stirr'd out of this place!
Nay, said I, I had it in Lady Betty's chamber, that's a plain case.
So Mary got me to bed, and cover'd me up warm,
However, she stole away my garters, that I might do myself no harm:
So I tumbl'd and toss'd all night, as you may very well think,
But hardly ever set my eyes together, or slept a wink.
So I was a-dream'd, methought, that we went and search'd the
        folks round,
And in a corner of Mrs Duke's box, tied in a rag, the money was
        found.
So next morning we told Whittle, and he fell a swearing;
Then my dame Wadgar came, and she, you know, is thick of hearing;

Dame, said I, as loud as I could bawl, do you know what a loss I
have had?
Nay, said she, my Lord Collway's folks are all very sad,
For my Lord Dromedary comes a Tuesday without fail;
Pugh! said I, but that's not the business that I ail.
Says Cary, says he, I have been a servant this five and twenty years,
come spring,
And in all the places I liv'd, I never heard of such a thing.
Yes, says the steward, I remember when I was at my Lady Shrews-
bury's,
Such a thing as this happen'd, just about the time of gooseberries.
So I went to the party suspected, and I found her full of grief;
(Now you must know, of all things in the world, I hate a thief).
However, I was resolv'd to bring the discourse slily about,
Mrs Dukes, said I, here's an ugly accident has happen'd out;
'Tis not that I value the money three skips of a louse;
But the thing I stand upon, is the credit of the house;
'Tis true, seven pound, four shillings, and six pence, makes a great
hole in my wages,
Besides, as they say, service is no inheritance in these ages.
Now, Mrs Dukes, you know, and every body understands,
That tho' 'tis hard to judge, yet money can't go without hands.
The devil take me, said she, (blessing her self,) if ever I saw't!
So she roar'd like a Bedlam, as tho' I had call'd her all to naught;
So you know, what could I say to her any more,
I e'en left her, and came away as wise as I was before.
Well: but then they would have had me gone to the cunning man;
No, said I, 'tis the same thing, the chaplain will be here anon.
So the chaplain came in. Now the servants say, he is my sweet-heart,
Because he's always in my chamber, and I always take his part;
So, as the Devil would have it, before I was aware, out I blunder'd,
Parson, said I, can you cast a nativity, when a body's plunder'd?
(Now, you must know, he hates to be call'd Parson, like the Devil.)
Truly, says he, Mrs Nab, it might become you to be more civil:
If your money be gone, as a learned Divine says, d'ye see,
You are no text for my handling, so take that from me:
I was never taken for a conjurer before, I'd have you to know.

Lord, said I, don't be angry, I am sure I never thought you so;
You know, I honour the cloth, I design to be a parson's wife,
I never took one in your coat for a conjurer in all my life.
With that, he twisted his girdle at me like a rope, as who should say,
Now you may go hang your self for me, and so went away.
Well; I thought I should have swoon'd: Lord, said I, what shall I do?
I have lost my money, and I shall lose my true-love too.
So, my lord call'd me; Harry, said my lord, don't cry,
I'll give something towards thy loss; and says my Lady, so will I.
Oh but, said I, what if after all the chaplain won't *come to*?
For that, he said, (an't please your Excellencies) I must petition you.

The premises tenderly consider'd, I desire your Excellencies' pro-
        tection,
And that I may have a share in next Sunday's collection:
And over and above, that I may have your Excellencies' letter,
With an order for the chaplain aforesaid; or instead of him, a better:
And then your poor petitioner, both night and day,
Or the chaplain, (for 'tis his trade) as in duty bound, shall ever pray.

VERSES said to be written on the UNION

The queen has lately lost a part
Of her entirely-*English* heart,
For want of which by way of botch,
She piec'd it up again with *Scotch*.
Blest revolution, which creates
Divided hearts, united states.
See how the double nation lies;
Like a rich coat with skirts of frize:
As if a man in making posies
Should bundle thistles up with roses
Whoever yet a union saw
Of kingdoms, without faith or law.
Henceforward let no statesman dare,
A kingdom to a ship compare;

Lest he should call our commonweal,
A vessel with a double keel:
Which just like ours, new rigg'd and mann'd,
And got about a league from land,
By change of wind to leeward side
The pilot knew not how to guide.
So tossing faction will o'erwhelm
Our crazy double-bottom'd realm.

EPITAPH ON PARTRIDGE

Here five foot deep lies on his back
A cobbler, starmonger, and quack,
Who to the stars in pure good-will,
Does to his best look upward still.
Weep all you customers that use
His pills, his almanacs, or shoes.
And you that did your fortunes seek,
Step to this grave but once a week,
This earth which bears his body's print,
You'll find has so much virtue in't,
That I durst pawn my ears, 'twill tell
Whate'er concerns you full as well,
In physick, stolen goods, or love,
As he himself could, when above.

A DESCRIPTION OF THE MORNING

Now hardly here and there a Hackney-coach
Appearing, show'd the ruddy morn's approach.
Now Betty from her master's bed had flown,
And softly stole to discompose her own. .
The slipshod prentice from his master's door,
Had par'd the dirt, and sprinkled round the floor.
Now Moll had whirl'd her mop with dext'rous airs,

Prepar'd to scrub the entry and the stairs.
The youth with broomy stumps began to trace
The kennel-edge, where wheels had worn the place.
The smallcoal-man was heard with cadence deep,
'Till drown'd in shriller notes of chimney-sweep.
Duns at his Lordship's gate began to meet,
And brickdust Moll had scream'd through half a street.
The turnkey now his flock returning sees,
Duly let out a nights to steal for fees.
The watchful bailiffs take their silent stands,
And school-boys lag with satchels in their hands.

A DESCRIPTION OF A CITY SHOWER

Careful observers may foretell the hour
(By sure prognostics) when to dread a show'r:
While rain depends, the pensive cat gives o'er
Her frolics, and pursues her tail no more.
Returning home at night, you'll find the sink
Strike your offended sense with double stink.
If you be wise, then go not far to dine,
You spend in coach-hire more than save in wine.
A coming show'r your shooting corns presage,
Old aches throb, your hollow tooth will rage.
Sauntering in coffee-house is Dullman seen;
He damns the climate, and complains of spleen.

Mean while the south rising with dabbled wings,
A sable cloud a-thwart the welkin flings,
That swill'd more liquor than it could contain,
And like a drunkard gives it up again.
Brisk Susan whips her linen from the rope,
While the first drizzling show'r is born aslope,
Such is that sprinkling which some careless quean
Flirts on you from her mop, but not so clean.
You fly, invoke the Gods; then turning, stop

To rail; she singing, still whirls on her mop.
Not yet, the dust had shunn'd th' unequal strife,
But aided by the wind, fought still for life;
And wafted with its foe by violent gust,
'Twas doubtful which was rain, and which was dust.
Ah! where must needy poet seek for aid,
When dust and rain at once his coat invade;
Sole coat, where dust cemented by the rain,
Erects the nap, and leaves a cloudy stain.

Now in contiguous drops the flood comes down,
Threat'ning with deluge this *devoted* town.
To shops in crowds the dagled females fly,
Pretend to cheapen goods, but nothing buy.
The templer spruce, while ev'ry spout's a-broach,
Stays till 'tis fair, yet seems to call a coach.
The tuck'd-up sempstress walks with hasty strides,
While streams run down her oil'd umbrella's sides.
Here various kinds by various fortunes led,
Commence acquaintance underneath a shed.
Triumphant Tories, and desponding Whigs,
Forget their feuds, and join to save their wigs.
Boxed in a chair the beau impatient sits,
While spouts run clatt'ring o'er the roof by fits;
And ever and anon with frightful din
The leather sounds, he trembles from within.
So when Troy chair-men bore the wooden steed,
Pregnant with Greeks, impatient to be freed,
(Those bully Greeks, who, as the moderns do,
Instead of paying chair-men, run them thro').
Laoco'n struck the outside with his spear,
And each imprison'd hero quak'd for fear.

Now from all parts the swelling kennels flow,
And bear their trophies with them as they go:
Filth of all hues and odours seem to tell
What streets they sail'd from, by the sight and smell.

They, as each torrent drives, with rapid force
From Smithfield, or St Pulchre's shape their course,
And in huge confluent join at Snow-Hill Ridge,
Fall from the conduit prone to Holborn-Bridge.
Sweepings from butchers' stalls, dung, guts, and blood,
Drown'd puppies, stinking sprats, all drench'd in mud,
Dead cats and turnip-tops come tumbling down the flood.

CORINNA

This day, (the year I dare not tell,)
   Apollo play'd the midwife's part,
Into the world Corinna fell,
   And he endowed her with his art.

But Cupid with a satyr comes;
   Both softly to the cradle creep:
Both stroke her hands, and rub her gums,
   While the poor child lay fast asleep.

Then Cupid thus: This little maid
   Of Love shall always speak and write;
And I pronounce, (the satyr said)
   The world shall feel her scratch and bite.

Her talent she display'd betimes;
   For in twice twelve revolving moons,
She seem'd to laugh and squall in rhymes,
   And all her gestures were lampoons.

At six years old, the subtle jade
   Stole to the pantry-door, and found
The butler with my Lady's maid;
   And you may swear the tale went round.

She made a song, how little Miss
   Was kiss'd and slobber'd by a lad:

And how, when Master went to piss,
  Miss came, and peep'd at all he had.

At twelve, a poet, and coquette;
  Marries for Love, half whore, half wife;
Cuckolds, elopes, and runs in debt;
  Turns auth'ress, and is Curll's for life.

HORACE, Lib. 2. Sat. 6 (part of it imitated)

I often wish'd, that I had clear
For life, six hundred pounds a year,
A handsome house to lodge a friend,
A river at my garden's end,
A terrace walk, and half a rood
Of land set out to plant a wood.

  Well, now I have all this and more,
I ask not to increase my store,
And should be perfectly content,
Could I but live on this side Trent;
Nor cross the Channel twice a year,
To spend six months with statesmen here.

  I must by all means come to town,
'Tis for the service of the Crown.
'Lewis; the Dean will be of use,
Send for him up, take no excuse.'
The toil, the danger of the seas;
Great ministers ne'er think of these;
Or let it cost five hundred pound,
No matter where the money's found;
It is but so much more in debt,
And that they ne'er considered yet.

  'Good Mr Dean go change your gown,
Let my lord know you're come to town.'

I hurry me in haste away,
Not thinking it is Levee-day;
And find his honour in a pound,
Hemm'd by a triple circle round,
Chequer'd with ribbons blue and green;
How should I thrust myself between?
Some wag observes me thus perplext,
And smiling, whispers to the next,
'I thought the Dean had been too proud,
To jostle here among a crowd.'
Another in a surly fit,
Tells me I have more zeal than wit,
'So eager to express your love,
You ne'er consider whom you shove,
But rudely press before a duke.'
I own, I'm pleas'd with this rebuke,
And take it kindly meant to show
What I desire the world should know.

    I get a whisper, and withdraw,
When twenty fools I never saw
Come with petitions fairly penn'd,
Desiring I would stand their friend.

    This, humbly offers me his case:
That, begs my interest for a place.
A hundred other men's affairs
Like bees, are humming in my ears.
'To morrow my appeal comes on,
Without your help the cause is gone—'
The Duke expects my lord and you,
About some great affair, at two—
'Put my Lord Bolingbroke in mind,
To get my warrant quickly signed:
Consider, 'tis my first request.—'
Be satisfied, I'll do my best:—
Then presently he falls to tease,

'You may for certain, if you please;
I doubt not, if his Lordship knew—
And Mr Dean, one word from you—'

'Tis (let me see) three years and more,
(October next, it will be four)
Since Harley bid me first attend,
And chose me for an humble friend;
Would take me in his coach to chat,
And question me of this and that;
As 'What's a-clock?' And, 'How's the wind?
Whose chariot's that we left behind?'
Or gravely try to read the lines
Writ underneath the country signs;
Or, 'Have you nothing new to day
From Pope, from Parnel, or from Gay?'
Such tattle often entertains
My lord and me as far as Staines,
As once a week we travel down
To Windsor, and again to town,
Where all that passes, *inter nos*,
Might be proclaim'd at Charing-Cross.

Yet some I know with envy swell,
Because they see me us'd so well:
'How think you of our friend the Dean?
I wonder what some people mean;
My Lord and he are grown so great,
Always together, *tête à tête*:
What, they admire him for his jokes—
See but the fortune of some folks!'
There flies about a strange report
Of some express arriv'd at court;
I'm stopt by all the fools I meet,
And catechis'd in ev'ry street.
'You, Mr Dean frequent the great;
Inform us, will the Emp'ror treat?

Or do the prints and papers lie?'
Faith sir, you know as much as I.
'Ah Doctor, how you love to jest?
'Tis now no secret'—I protest
'Tis one to me.—'Then, tell us, pray
When are the troops to have their pay?'
And, though I solemnly declare
I know no more than my Lord Mayor,
They stand amaz'd, and think me grown
The closest mortal ever known.

Thus in a sea of folly tost,
My choicest hours of life are lost:
Yet always wishing to retreat;
Oh, could I see my country seat.
There leaning near a gentle brook,
Sleep, or peruse some ancient book;
And there in sweet oblivion drown
Those cares that haunt a court and town.

Mary the Cook-Maid's LETTER to Dr Sheridan

Well; if ever I saw such another man since my mother bound my head,
You a gentleman! marry come up, I wonder where you were bred?
I am sure such words does not become a man of your cloth,
I would not give such language to a dog, faith and troth.
Yes; you call'd my master a knave: fie Mr Sheridan, 'tis a shame
For a parson, who shou'd know better things, to come out with such
            a name.
Knave in your teeth, Mr Sheridan, 'tis both a shame and a sin,
And the Dean my master is an honester man than you and all your
            kin:
He has more goodness in his little finger, than you have in your
            whole body,
My master is a parsonable man, and not a spindle-shank'd hoddy
            doddy.

And now whereby I find you would fain make an excuse,
Because my master one day in anger call'd you goose.
Which, and I am sure I have been his servant four years since October,
And he never call'd me worse than sweet-heart drunk or sober:
Not that I know his Reverence was ever concern'd to my knowledge,
Tho' you and your come-rogues keep him out so late in your wicked
      college.

You say you will eat grass on his grave: a Christian eat grass!
Whereby you now confess your self to be a goose or an ass:
But that's as much as to say, that my Master should die before ye,
Well, well, that's as God pleases, and I don't believe that's a true
      story,
And so say I told you so, and you may go tell my Master; what care I?
And I don't care who knows it, 'tis all one to Mary.
Every body knows, that I love to tell truth and shame the Devil,
I am but a poor servant, but I think gentle folks should be civil.
Besides, you found fault with our vittles one day that you was here,
I remember it was upon a Tuesday, of all days in the year.
And Saunders the man says, you are always jesting and mocking,
Mary said he, (one day, as I was mending my Master's stocking,)
My Master is so fond of that minister that keeps the school;
I thought my Master a wise man, but that man makes him a fool.
Saunders said I, I would rather than a quart of ale,
He would come into our kitchen, and I would pin a dishclout to his
      tail.
And now I must go, and get Saunders to direct this letter,
For I write but a sad scrawl, but my sister Marget she writes better.
Well, but I must run and make the bed before my Master comes
      from pray'rs,
And see now, it strikes ten, and I hear him coming up stairs:
Whereof I cou'd say more to your verses, if I could write written
      hand,
And so I remain in a civil way, your servant to command,
                              Mary.

ON STELLA'S BIRTH-DAY

Stella this day is thirty four,
(We shan't dispute a year or more)
However Stella, be not troubled,
Although thy size and years are doubled,
Since first I saw thee at sixteen
The brightest virgin on the green,
So little is thy form declin'd
Made up so largely in thy mind.
Oh, would it please the gods to split
Thy beauty, size, and years, and wit,
No age could furnish out a pair
Of nymphs so graceful, wise and fair
With half the lustre of your eyes,
With half your wit, your years and size:
And then before it grew too late,
How should I beg of gentle fate,
(That either nymph might have her swain,)
To split my worship too in twain.

A QUIET LIFE, AND A GOOD NAME

Nell scolded in so loud a din
That Will durst hardly venture in;
He mark't the conjugal dispute,
Nell roar'd incessant, Dick sate mute:
But when he saw his friend appear
Cried bravely, patience, good my dear.
At sight of Will she bawl'd no more,
But hurried out, and clapp't the door.
  Why Dick! the Devil's in thy Nell
Quoth Will; thy house is worse than hell:
Why, what a peal the jade has rung,
Damn her, why don't you slit her tongue?
For nothing else will make it cease,—

Dear Will, I suffer this for peace;
I never quarrel with my wife,
I bear it for a quiet life
Scripture you know exhorts us to it,
Bids us to seek peace and ensue it.
   Will went again to visit Dick
And entring in the very nick,
He saw virago Nell belabour
With Dick's own staff his peaceful neighbour,
Poor Will, who needs must interpose,
Receiv'd a brace or two of blows.
   But now, to make my story short
Will drew out Dick to take a quart,
Why Dick, thy wife has dev'lish whims:
Ods buds, why don't you break her limbs:
If she were mine, and had such tricks,
I'd teach her how to handle sticks:
Zounds I would ship her for Jamaica
And truck the carrion for Tobacca,
I'd send her far enough away—
Dear Will, but, what would people say?
Lord! I should get so ill a name,
The neighbours round would cry out shame.
   Dick suffer'd for his peace and credit,
But who believ'd him when he said it:
Can he who makes himself a slave
Consult his peace, or credit save?
Dick found it by his ill success
His quiet small, his credit less;
Nell serv'd him at the usu'l rate
She stunn'd, and then she broke his pate.
And what he thought the hardest case,
The parish jeer'd him to his face:
Those men who wore the breeches least
Call'd him a cuckold, fool, and beast,
At home, he was pursu'd with noise,
Abroad, was pester'd by the boys,

Within, his wife would break his bones,
Without, they pelted him with stones,
The prentices procur'd a riding
To act his patience, and her chiding.
    False patience, and mistaken pride!
There are ten thousand Dicks beside;
Slaves to their quiet and good name,
Are us'd like Dick, and bear the blame.

PHILLIS, Or, the Progress of Love

Desponding Phillis was endu'd
With ev'ry talent of a prude,
She trembled when a man drew near;
Salute her, and she turn'd her ear:
If o'er against her you were plac't
She durst not look above your waist;
She'd rather take you to her bed
Than let you see her dress her head;
In church you heard her through the crowd
Repeat the Absolution loud;
In church, secure behind her fan
She durst behold that monster, Man:
There practis'd how to place her head,
And bit her lips to make them red:
Or on the mat devoutly kneeling
Would lift her eyes up to the ceiling,
And heave her bosom unaware
For neighb'ring beaux to see it bare.
    At length a lucky lover came,
And found admittance to the dame.
Suppose all parties now agreed,
The writings drawn, the lawyer fee'd,
The vicar and the ring bespoke:
Guess how could such a match be broke.
See then what mortals place their bliss in!

31

Next morn betimes the bride was missing,
The mother scream'd, the father chid,
Where can this idle wench be hid?
No news of Phil. The bridegroom came,
And thought his bride had sculk't for shame,
Because her father us'd to say
The girl had such a bashful way.
   Now John the Butler must be sent
To learn the road that Phillis went;
The groom was wisht to saddle Crop,
For John must neither light nor stop;
But find her where so'er she fled,
And bring her back, alive or dead.
See here again the Dev'l to do;
For truly John was missing too:
The horse and pillion both were gone
Phillis, it seems, was fled with John.
Old Madam who went up to find
What papers Phil had left behind,
A letter on the toilet sees
To my much honour'd father; These:
('Tis always done, romances tell us,
When daughters run away with fellows)
Fill'd with the choicest common-places,
By others us'd in the like cases.
That, long ago a fortune-teller
Exactly said what now befell her,
And in a glass had made her see
A serving-man of low degree:
It was her fate; must be forgiven;
For marriages were made in heaven:
His pardon begg'd, but to be plain,
She'd do't if 'twere to do again.
Thank God, 'twas neither shame nor sin,
For John was come of honest kin:
Love never thinks of rich and poor,
She'd beg with John from door to door:

Forgive her, if it be a crime,
She'll never do't another time,
She ne'er before in all her life
Once disobey'd him, maid nor wife.
One argument she summ'd up all in,
The thing was done and past recalling:
And therefore hop'd she should recover
His favour, when his passion's over.
She valued not what others thought her;
And was—his most obedient daughter.

Fair maidens all attend the Muse
Who now the wandring pair pursues:
Away they rode in homely sort
Their journey long, their money short;
The loving couple well bemir'd,
The horse and both the riders tir'd:
Their vittles bad, their lodging worse,
Phil cried, and John began to curse;
Phil wish't, that she had strained a limb
When first she ventur'd out with him.
John wish't, that he had broke a leg
When first for her he quitted Peg.

But what adventures more befell 'em
The Muse hath now no time to tell 'em.
How Johnny wheedled, threatened, fawn'd,
Till Phillis all her trinkets pawn'd:
How oft she broke her marriage vows
In kindness to maintain her spouse;
Till swains unwholesome spoil'd the trade,
For now the surgeon must be paid;
To whom those perquisites are gone
In Christian justice due to John.

When food and raiment now grew scarce
Fate put a period to the farce;
And with exact poetic justice:
For John is landlord, Phillis Hostess;
They keep at Staines the old blue Boar,
Are cat and dog, and rogue and whore.

33

THE PROGRESS OF BEAUTY

When first Diana leaves her bed
Vapours and steams her looks disgrace,
A frowzy dirty colour'd red
Sits on her cloudy wrinkled face.

  But by degrees when mounted high
Her artificial face appears
Down from her window in the sky,
Her spots are gone, her visage clears.

  'Twixt earthly females and the moon
All parallels exactly run;
If Celia should appear too soon
Alas, the nymph would be undone.

  To see her from her pillow rise
All reeking in a cloudy steam,
Crack'd lips, foul teeth, and gummy eyes,
Poor Strephon, how would he blaspheme!

  Three colours, black, and red, and white,
So graceful in their proper place,
Remove them to a different light
They form a frightful hideous face,

  For instance; when the lily skips
Into the precincts of the rose,
And takes possession of the lips,
Leaving the purple to the nose.

  So Celia went entire to bed,
All her complexions safe and sound,
But when she rose, white, black and red
Though still in sight, had chang'd their ground.

The black, which would not be confin'd
A more inferior station seeks
Leaving the fiery red behind,
And mingles in her muddy cheeks.

But Celia can with ease reduce
By help of pencil, paint and brush
Each colour to its place and use,
And tea'ch her cheeks again to blush.

She knows her early self no more,
But fill'd with admiration, stands,
As other painters oft adore
The workmanship of their own hands.

Thus after four important hours
Celia's the wonder of her sex;
Say, which among the heav'nly pow'rs
Could cause such marvellous effects?

Venus, indulgent to her kind
Gave women all their hearts could wish
When first she taught them where to find
White lead, and Lusitanian dish.

Love with white lead cements his wings,
White lead was sent us to repair
The brightest, brittlest earthly things
A lady's face, and China ware.

She ventures now to lift the sash,
The window is her proper sphere;
Ah lovely nymph be not too rash,
Nor let the beaux approach too near.

Take pattern by your sister star,
Delude at once and bless our sight,

When you are seen, be seen from far,
And chiefly choose to shine by night.

　But, art no longer can prevail
When the materials all are gone,
The best mechanic hand must fail
Where nothing's left to work upon.

　Matter, as wise logicians say,
Cannot without a form subsist,
And form, say I, as well as they,
Must fail if matter brings no grist.

　And this is fair Diana's case
For, all astrologers maintain
Each night a bit drops off her face
When mortals say she's in her wane.

　While Partridge wisely shows the cause
Efficient of the moon's decay,
That cancer with his pois'nous claws
Attacks her in the milky way:

　But Gadbury in art profound
From her pale cheeks pretends to show
That swain Endymion is not sound,
Or else, that Mercury's her foe.

　But, let the cause be what it will,
In half a month she looks so thin
That Flamstead can with all his skill
See but her forehead and her chin.

　Yet as she wastes, she grows discreet,
Till midnight never shows her head;
So rotting Celia strolls the street
When sober folks are all a-bed.

For sure if this be Luna's fate,
Poor Celia, but of mortal race
In vain expects a longer date
To the materials of her face.

When Mercury her tresses mows
To think of black-head combs is vain,
No painting can restore a nose,
Nor will her teeth return again.

Ye pow'rs who over love preside,
Since mortal beauties drop so soon,
If you would have us well supplied,
Send us new nymphs with each new moon.

EPITAPH ON DEMAR

Beneath this verdant hillock lies
Demar the wealthy, and the wise.
His heirs that he might safely rest,
Have put his carcass in a chest.
The very chest, in which they say
His other self, his money lay.
And if his heirs continue kind,
To that dear self he left behind;
I dare believe that four in five
Will think his better self alive.

'DORINDA DREAMS...'

Dorinda dreams of dress a bed
  'Tis all her thought and art,
Her lace hath got within her head
  Her stays stick to her heart.

THE DESCRIPTION OF AN IRISH FEAST, TRANSLATED ALMOST LITERALLY OUT OF THE ORIGINAL IRISH

O'Rourk's noble fare
  Will ne'er be forgot,
By those who were there,
  Or those who were not.
His revels to keep,
  We sup and we dine,
On seven score sheep,
  Fat bullocks and swine.
Usquebaugh to our feast
  In pails was brought up,
An hundred at least,
  And a madder our cup.
O there is the sport,
  We rise with the light,
In disorderly sort,
  From snoring all night.
O how was I trick't,
  My pipe it was broke,
My pocket was pick't,
  I lost my new cloak.
I'm rifled, quoth Nell,
  Of mantle and kercher,
Why then fare them well,
  The de'il take the searcher.
Come, Harper, strike up,
  But first by your favour,
Boy, give us a cup;
  Ay, this has some savour:
O'Rourk's jolly boys
  Ne'er dream't of the matter,
Till rous'd by the noise,
  And musical clatter,
They bounce from their nest,
  No longer will tarry,

They rise ready drest,
  Without one *Ave Mary*.
They dance in a round,
  Cutting capers and ramping,
A mercy the ground
  Did not burst with their stamping.
The floor is all wet
  With leaps and with jumps,
While the water and sweat,
  Splish, splash in their pumps.
Bless you late and early,
  Laughlin O Enagin,
By my hand, you dance rarely,
  Margery Grinagin.
Bring straw for our bed,
  Shake it down to the feet,
Then over us spread
  The winnowing sheet.
To show, I don't flinch,
  Fill the bowl up again,
Then give us a pinch
  Of your sneezing; *a Yean*.
Good lord, what a sight,
  After all their good cheer,
For people to fight
  In the midst of their beer:
They rise from their feast,
  And hot are their brains,
A cubit at least
  The length of their skeans.
What stabs and what cuts,
  What clatt'ring of sticks,
What strokes on the guts,
  What bastings and kicks!
With cudgels of oak,
  Well harden'd in flame,
An hundred heads broke,

An hundred struck lame.
You churl, I'll maintain
  My father built Lusk,
The Castle of Slain,
  And Carrickdrumrusk:
The Earl of Kildare,
  And Moynalta, his brother,
As great as they are,
  I was nurs'd by their mother.
Ask that of old Madam,
  She'll tell you who's who,
As far up as Adam,
  She knows it is true,
Come down with that beam,
  If cudgels are scarce,
A blow on the weam,
  Or a kick on the arse.

THE JOURNAL

Thalia, tell in sober lays,
How George, Nim, Dan, Dean pass their days;
Begin, my Muse, first from our bowers,
We issue forth at different hours;
At seven, the Dean in night-gown drest,
Goes round the house to wake the rest:
At nine, grave Nim and George facetious,
Go to the dean to read Lucretius.
At ten, my lady comes and hectors,
And kisses George, and ends our lectures:
And when she has him by the neck fast,
Hauls him, and scolds us down to breakfast.
We squander there an hour or more,
And then all hands, boys, to the oar
All, Heteroclite Dan except,
Who never time nor order kept.

But by peculiar whimsies drawn,
Peeps in the ponds to look for spawn:
O'er sees the work, or Dragon rows,
Or mars a text, or mends his hose.
Or—but proceed we in our *Journal*,—
At two or after we return all,
From the four elements assembling,
Warn'd by the bell, all folks come trembling,
From airy garrets some descend,
Some from the lake's remotest end.
My lord and Dean, the fire forsake;
Dan leaves the earthly spade and rake,
The loit'rers quake, no corner hides them,
And lady Betty soundly chides them.
Now water's brought, and dinner's done,
With Church and King, the lady's gone;
Not reckoning half an hour we pass,
In talking o'er a moderate glass.
Dan growing drowsy like a thief,
Steals off to doze away his beef,
And this must pass for reading Hammond:
While George, and Dean, go to Back-Gammon.
George, Nim and Dean, set out at four,
And then again, boys, to the oar.
But when the sun goes to the deep,
Not to disturb him in his sleep;
Or make a rumbling o'er his head,
His candle out, and he a-bed.
We watch his motions to a minute,
And leave the flood when he goes in it:
Now stinted in the short'ning day,
We go to pray'rs, and then to play
Till supper comes, and after that,
We sit an hour to drink and chat.
'Tis late, the old and younger pairs,
By Adam lighted walk up stairs:
The weary Dean goes to his chamber,

And Nim and Dan to garret clamber:
So when this circle we have run,
The curtain falls, and all is done.
I might have mention'd several facts,
Like episodes between the acts;
And tell who loses, and who wins,
Who gets a cold, who breaks his shins.
How Dan caught nothing in his net,
And how the boat was over set,
For brevity I have retrench'd,
How in the lake the Dean was drench'd:
It would be an exploit to brag on,
How valiant George rode o'er the Dragon;
How steady in the storm he sat,
And sav'd his oar, but lost his hat.

THE PROGRESS OF MARRIAGE

Aetatis suae fifty two
A rich divine began to woo
A handsome young imperious girl
Nearly related to an earl.
Her parents and her friends consent,
The couple to the temple went:
They first invite the Cyprian Queen,
'Twas answered, she would not be seen.
The Graces next, and all the Muses
Were bid in form, but sent excuses:
Juno attended at the porch
With farthing candle for a torch,
While mistress Iris held her train,
The faded bow distilling rain.
Then Hebe came and took her place
But showed no more than half her face
Whate'er these dire forebodings meant,
In mirth the wedding-day was spent.

The *wedding-day*, you take me right,
I promise nothing for the night:
The bridegroom dress'd, to make a figure,
Assumes an artificial vigour;
A flourisht night-cap on, to grace
His ruddy, wrinkled, smirking face,
Like the faint red upon a pippin
Half wither'd by a winter's keeping.
  And, thus set out this happy pair,
The swain is rich, the nymph is fair;
But, which I gladly would forget,
The swain is old, the nymph coquette.
Both from the goal together start;
Scarce run a step before they part;
No common ligament that binds
The various textures of their minds,
Their thoughts and actions, hopes and fears,
Less corresponding than their years.
Her spouse desires his coffee soon,
She rises to her tea at noon.
While he goes out to cheapen books,
She at the glass consults her looks
While Betty's buzzing at her ear,
Lord, what a dress these parsons wear,
So odd a choice, how could she make,
Wish't him a Colonel for her sake.
Then on her fingers' ends she counts
Exact to what his age amounts,
The Dean, she heard her uncle say
Is fifty, if he be a day;
His ruddy cheeks are no disguise;
You see the crows' feet round his eyes.
At one she rambles to the shops
To cheapen tea, and talk with fops.
Or calls a council of her maids
And tradesmen, to compare brocades.
Her weighty morning bus'ness o'er

Sits down to dinner just at four;
Minds nothing that is done or said,
Her ev'ning *work* so fills her head;
The Dean, who us'd to dine at one,
Is mawkish, and his stomach gone;
In thread-bare gown, would scarce a louse hold,
Looks like the chaplain of the household,
Beholds her from the chaplain's place
In French brocades and Flanders lace;
He wonders what employs her brain;
But never asks, or asks in vain;
His mind is full of other cares,
And in the sneaking parson's airs
Computes, that half a parish dues
Will hardly find his wife in shoes.
Canst thou imagine, dull divine,
'Twill gain her love to make her fine?
Hath she no other wants beside?
You raise desire as well as pride,
Enticing coxcombs to adore,
And teach her to despise thee more
If in her coach she'll condescend
To place him at the hinder end
Her hoop is hoist above his nose,
His odious gown would soil her clothes,
And drops him at the church, to pray
While she drives on to see the play.
He like an orderly divine
Comes home a quarter after nine,
And meets her hasting to the ball,
Her chairmen push him from the wall:
He enters in, and walks up stairs,
And calls the family to prayers,
Then goes alone to take his rest
In bed, where he can spare her best.
At five the footmen make a din,
Her ladyship is just come in,

The masquerade began at two,
She stole away with much ado,
And shall be chid this afternoon
For leaving company so soon;
She'll say, and she may truly say't
She can't abide to stay out late.

But now, though scarce a twelvemonth married,
His lady has twelve times miscarried,
The cause, alas, is quickly guesst,
The town has whisper'd round the jest:
Think on some remedy in time
You find his Rev'rence past his prime,
Already dwindled to a lath;
No other way but try the bath:
For Venus rising from the ocean
Infus'd a strong prolific potion,
That mixt with Achelous spring,
The *horned* flood, as poets sing:
Who with an English beauty smitten
Ran under ground from Greece to Britain,
The genial virtue with him brought,
And gave the nymph a plenteous draught;
Then fled, and left his horn behind
For husbands past their youth to find;
The nymph who still with passion burn'd,
Was to a boiling fountain turn'd,
Where childless wives crowd ev'ry morn
To drink in Achilous' horn.
And here the father often gains
That title by another's pains.

Hither, though much against his grain,
The Dean has carried lady Jane
He for a while would not consent,
But vow'd his money all was spent;
His money spent! a clownish reason?

45

And, must my lady slip her season?
The doctor with a double fee
Was *brib'd* to make the Dean agree.
   Here, all diversions of the place
Are *proper* in my lady's case
With which she patiently complies,
Merely because her friends advise;
His money and her time employs
In music, raffling-rooms, and toys,
Or in the *cross-bath* seeks an heir
Since others oft have found one there;
Where if the Dean by chance appears
It shames his cassock and his years
He keeps his distance in the gallery
Till banish'd by some coxcomb's raillery;
For, it would his character expose
To bath among the belles and beaux.

   So have I seen within a pen
Young ducklings, fostered by a hen;
But when let out, they run and muddle
As instinct leads them, in a puddle;
The sober hen not born to swim
With mournful note clocks round the brim.

   The dean with all his best endeavour
Gets not an heir, but gets a fever;
A victim to the last essays
Of vigour in declining days.
He dies, and leaves his mourning mate
(What could he less) his whole estate.

   The widow goes through all her forms;
New lovers now will come in swarms.
Oh, may I see her soon dispensing
Her favours to some broken ensign
Him let her marry for his face,

And only coat of tarnish'd lace;
To turn her naked out of doors,
And spend her jointure on his whores:
But for a parting present leave her
A rooted pox to last for ever.

STELLA'S DISTRESS on the 3rd fatal day of October 1723

(lines 1-22)
The winter now begins to frown;
Poor Stella must pack off to town.
From purling streams & fountains bubbling
To Liffey's filthy side in Dublin;
From wholesome exercise and air
To sossing in an elbow chair:
From stomach sharp, and hearty feeding
To piddle like a lady breeding.
From ruling there the household singly
To be directed here by Dingley.
From ev'ry day a lordly banquet
To half a joint, & God be thanked:
From every meal Pontac in plenty
To a sour pint one day in twenty.
From growing richer with good cheer,
And yet run out by starving here:
From Ford who thinks of nothing mean
To the poor doings of the Dean:
From Ford attending at her call
To visits of Archdeacon Wall.
Say, Stella, which you most repent
You e'er returned, or ever went?

'IN CHURCH YOUR GRANDSIRE CUT HIS THROAT...'

In church your grandsire cut his throat;
  To do the job too long he tarried,
He should have had my hearty vote,
  To cut his throat before he married.

TO QUILCA, a Country House in no very good Repair, where the supposed Author, and some of his Friends, spent a Summer, in the Year 1725

Let me my properties explain,
A rotten cabin, dropping rain;
Chimneys with scorn rejecting smoke;
Stools, tables, chairs, and bed-steads broke:
Here elements have lost their uses,
Air ripens not, nor earth produces:
In vain we make poor Sheelagh toil,
Fire will not roast, nor water boil.
Thro' all the valleys, hills, and plains,
The goddess *Want* in triumph reigns;
And her chief officers of state,
Sloth, Dirt and *Theft* around her wait.

ADVICE to the Grub-street Verse-Writers

Ye poets ragged and forlorn,
  Down from your garrets haste,
Ye rhymers, dead as soon as born,
  Not yet consign'd to paste;

I know a trick to make you thrive;
  O, 'tis a quaint device:
Your still-born poems shall revive,
  And scorn to wrap up spice.

Get all your verses printed fair,
  Then, let them well be dried;
And, Curl must have a special care
  To leave the margin wide.

Lend these to paper-sparing Pope;
  And, when he sits to write,
No letter with an envelope
  Could give him more delight.

When Pope has fill'd the margins round,
  Why, then recall your loan;
Sell them to Curl for fifty pound,
  And swear they are your own.

CLEVER TOM CLINCH GOING TO BE HANGED

As clever Tom Clinch, while the rabble was bawling,
Rode stately through Holborn, to die in his calling;
He stopped at the George for a bottle of sack,
And promis'd to pay for it when he'd come back.
His waistcoat and stockings, and breeches were white,
His cap had a new cherry ribbon to tie' t.
The maids to the doors and the balconies ran,
And said, lack-a-day! he's a proper young man.
But, as from the windows the ladies he spy'd,
Like a beau in the box, he bow'd low on each side;
And when his last speech the loud hawkers did cry,
He swore from his cart, it was all a damn'd lie.
The hangman for pardon fell down on his knee;
Tom gave him a kick in the guts for his fee.
Then said, I must speak to the people a little,
But I'll see you all damn'd before I will *whittle*.
My honest friend Wild, may he long hold his place,
He lengthen'd my life with a whole year of grace.
Take courage, dear comrades, and be not afraid,

Nor slip this occasion to follow your trade.
My conscience is clear, and my spirits are calm,
And thus I go off without pray'r-book or psalm.
Then follow the practice of clever Tom Clinch,
Who hung like a hero, and never would flinch.

AT THE SIGN OF THE FOUR CROSSES
To the Landlord

There hang three crosses at thy door:
Hang up thy wife, and she'll make four.

THE FURNITURE OF A WOMAN'S MIND

A set of phrases learnt by rote;
A passion for a scarlet-coat;
When at a play to laugh, or cry,
Yet cannot tell the reason why:
Never to hold her tongue a minute;
While all she prates has nothing in it.
Whole hours can with a coxcomb sit,
And take his nonsense all for wit:
Her learning mounts to read a song,
But, half the words pronouncing wrong;
Has ev'ry repartee in store,
She spoke ten thousand times before.
Can ready compliments supply
On all occasions, cut and dry.
Such hatred to a parson's gown,
The sight will put her in a swown.
For conversation well endu'd;
She calls it witty to be rude;
And, placing raillery in railing,
Will tell aloud your greatest failing;
Nor makes a scruple to expose

Your bandy leg, or crooked nose.
Can, at her morning tea, run o'er
The scandal of the day before.
Improving hourly in her skill,
To cheat and wrangle at quadrille.

In choosing lace a critic nice,
Knows to a groat the lowest price;
Can in her female clubs dispute
What lining best the silk will suit;
What colours each complexion match:
And where with art to place a patch.

If chance a mouse creeps in her sight,
Can finely counterfeit a fright;
So, sweetly screams if it comes near her,
She ravishes all hearts to hear her.
Can dext'rously her husband tease,
By taking fits whene'er she please:
By frequent practice learns the trick
At proper seasons to be sick;
Thinks nothing gives one airs so pretty;
At once creating love and pity.
If Molly happens to be careless,
And but neglects to warm her hair-lace,
She gets a cold as sure as death;
And vows she scarce can fetch her breath.
Admires how modest women can
Be so *robustious* like a man.

In party, furious to her power;
A bitter Whig, or Tory sour;
Her arguments directly tend
Against the side she would defend:
Will prove herself a Tory plain,
From principles the Whigs maintain;
And, to defend the Whiggish cause,
Her topics from the Tories draws.

O yes! If any man can find
More virtues in a woman's mind,
Let them be sent to Mrs Harding;
She'll pay the charges to a farthing:
Take notice, she has my commission
To add them in the next edition;
They may out-sell a better thing;
So, holla boys; God save the King.

AN ELEGY ON DICKY AND DOLLY

Under this stone, lies Dicky and Dolly,
Doll dying first, Dick grew melancholly,
For Dick without Doll thought living a folly.

Dick lost in Doll, a wife tender and dear,
But Dick lost by Doll, twelve hundred a year,
A loss that Dick thought, no mortal could bear.

Dick sighed for his Doll and his mournful arms cross'd,
Thought much of his Doll, and the jointure he lost,
The first vex'd him much, but the other vex'd most.

Thus loaded with grief, Dick sigh'd and he cried,
To live without both full three months he tried,
But lik'd neither loss and so quietly died.

One bed while alive held both Doll and Dick
One coach oft carried them when they were quick,
One grave now contains them both *haec et hic.*

Dick left a pattern few will copy after,
Then Reader pray shed some tears of salt water,
For so sad a tale is no subject of laughter.

Meath smiles for his jointure, though gotten, so late,
The son laughs that got, the hard gotten estate,
And Cuffe grins for getting, the Alicant plate.

Here quiet they lie, in hopes to rise one day,
Both solemnly put, in this hole on a Sunday,
And here rest, *Sic transit gloria mundi.*

MAD MULLINIX AND TIMOTHY

M. I own 'tis not my bread and butter,
But prithee Tim, why all this clutter?
Why ever in these raging fits,
Damning to hell the Jacobits?
When, if you search the Kingdom round,
There's hardly twenty to be found;
No, not among the priests and friars.
  T. 'Twixt you and me God damn the liars.
  M. The Tories are gone ev'ry man over
To our illustrious House of Hanover.
From all their conduct this is plain,
And then— *T.* God damn the liars again.
Did not an earl but lately vote
To bring in (I could cut his throat)
Our whole account of public debts.
  M. Lord how this frothy coxcomb frets! *(aside)*
  T. Did not an able statesman Bishop
This dangerous horrid motion dish up?
As Popish craft? Did he not rail on't?
Show fire and faggot in the tail on't?
Proving the earl a grand offender,
And in a plot for the Pretender?
Whose fleet, in all our friends' opinion,
Was then embarking at Avignon.
  M. These brangling jars of Whig and Tory,
Are stale, and worn as Troy-town story.

The wrong 'tis certain you were both in,
And now you find you fought for nothing.
Your faction, when their game was new,
Might want such noisy fools as you;
But you when all the show is past
Resolve to stand it out the last;
Like Martin Marrall, gaping on,
Not minding when the song was done.
When all the bees are gone to settle,
You clutter still your brazen kettle.
The leaders whom you listed under,
Have dropt their arms, and seiz'd the plunder.
And when the war is past you come
To rattle in their eyes your drum.
And, as that hateful hideous Grecian
Thirsites (he was your relation)
Was more abhorr'd, and scorn'd by those
With whom he serv'd, than by his foes,
So thou art grown the detestation
Of all thy party through the nation.
Thy peevish, and perpetual teasing,
With plots; and Jacobites and treason;
Thy busy never-meaning face;
Thy screw'd up front; thy state grimace;
Thy formal nods; important sneers;
Thy whisp'rings foisted in all ears;
(Which are, whatever you may think,
But nonsense wrapt up in a stink)
Have made thy presence in a true sense,
To thy own side so damn'd a nuisance,
That when they have you in their eye,
As if the Devil drove, they fly.
   T. My good friend Mullinix forbear.
I vow to God you're too severe.
If it could ever yet be known
I took advice except my own,
It should be yours. But damn my blood

I must pursue the public good.
The faction, (is it not notorious?)
Keck at the memory of Glorious.
'Tis true, nor need I to be told,
My quondam friends are grown so cold,
That scarce a creature can be found,
To prance with me his statue round.
The public safety I foresee,
Henceforth depends alone on me.
And while this vital breath I blow,
Or from above, or from below,
I'll sputter, swagger, curse and rail,
The Tories' terror, scourge and flail.
   M. Tim, you mistake the matter quite,
The Tories! you are their delight.
And should you act, a diff'rent part,
Be grave and wise, 'twould break their heart.
Why, Tim, you have a taste I know,
And often see a puppet-show.
Observe, the audience is in pain,
While Punch is hid behind the scene,
But when they hear his rusty voice,
With what impatience they rejoice.
And then they value not two straws,
How Solomon decides the cause,
Which the true mother, which pretender,
Nor listen to the witch of Endor;
Should Faustus, with the Devil behind him,
Enter the stage they never mind him;
If Punch, to spur their fancy, shows
In at the door his monstrous nose,
Then sudden draws it back again,
O what a pleasure mixt with pain!
You ev'ry moment think an age,
Till he appears upon the stage.
And first his bum you see him clap,
Upon the Queen of Sheba's lap.

The Duke of Lorrain drew his sword,
Punch roaring ran, and running roar'd.
Reviles all people in his jargon,
And sells the King of Spain a bargain.
St George himself he plays the wag on,
And mounts astride upon the dragon.
He gets a thousand thumps and kicks
Yet cannot leave his roguish tricks;
In every action thrusts his nose
The reason why no mortal knows.
In doleful scenes, that break our heart,
Punch comes, like you, and lets a fart.
There's not a puppet made of wood,
But what wou'd hang him if they cou'd.
While teasing all, by all he's teas'd,
How well are the spectators pleas'd!
Who in the motion have no share;
But purely come to hear, and stare;
Have no concern for Sabra's sake,
Which gets the better, Saint, or Snake.
Provided Punch (for there's the jest)
Be soundly maul'd, and plagues the rest.
  Thus Tim, philosophers suppose,
The world consists of puppet-shows;
Where petulant, conceited fellows
Perform the part of Punchinellos;
So at this booth, which we call Dublin,
Tim thou'rt the Punch to stir up trouble in;
You wriggle, fidge, and make a rout
Put all your brother puppets out,
Run on in one perpetual round,
To tease, perplex, disturb, confound,
Intrude with monkey grin, and clatter
To interrupt all serious matter,
Are grown the nuisance of your clan,
Who hate and scorn you, to a man;
But then the lookers on, the Tories

You still divert with merry stories;
They would consent, that all the crew
Were hanged, before they'd part with you.
　But tell me, Tim, upon the spot,
By all this coil what hast thou got?
If Tories must have all the sport,
I feel you'll be disgrac'd at Court.
　T. Got? Damn my blood *I frank my letters,*
Walk by my place, before my betters,
And simple as I now stand here,
Expect in time, to be a peer;
Got? Damn me, why I got my will!
Ne'er hold my peace, and ne'er stand still.
I fart with twenty ladies by;
They call me beast, and what care I?
I bravely call the Tories jacks,
And sons of whores—behind their backs.
But could you bring me once to think,
That when I strut, and stare, and stink,
Revile and slander, fume and storm,
Betray, make oath, impeach, inform,
With such a constant, loyal zeal,
To serve my self and common-weal,
And fret the Tories' souls to death,
I did but lose my precious breath,
And when I damn my soul to plague 'em,
Am, as you tell me, but their may-game,
Consume my vitals! they shall know,
I am not to be treated so,
I'd rather hang my self by half,
Than give those rascals cause to laugh.
　But how, my friend, can I endure
Once so renown'd to live obscure?
No little boys and girls to cry
There's nimble Tim a passing by.
No more my dear delightful way tread,
Of keeping up *a party hatred.*

Will none the Tory dogs pursue,
When through the streets I cry *hulloo*?
Must all my dammee's, bloods and wounds
Pass only now for empty sounds?
Shall Tory rascals be elected,
Although I swear them disaffected?
And when I roar *a Plot, a Plot*,
Will our own party mind me not?
So qualified to swear and lie,
Will they not trust me for a spy?
Dear Mullinix, your good advice
I beg, you see the case is nice,
O, were I equal in renown,
Like thee, to please this thankless town!
Or blest with such engaging parts,
To win the truant school-boys' hearts!
Thy virtues meet their just reward,
Attended by the Sable-guard,
Charm'd by thy voice the 'prentice drops
The snow-ball destin'd at thy chops;
Thy graceful steps, and colonel's air
Allure the cinder-picking fair.

M. No more—In mark of true affection
I take thee under my protection.
Thy parts are good, 'tis not denied,
I wish they had been well applied.
But now observe my counsel (*viz*)
Adapt your habit to your phiz.
You must no longer thus equip 'ye
As Horace says, *Optat ephippia.*
(There's Latin too that you may see
How I improv'd by Dr Lee)
I have a coat at home, that you may try,
'Tis just like this, which hangs by geometry.
My hat has much the nicer air,
Your block will fit it to a hair.
That wig, I wou'd not for the world

58

Have it so formal, and so curl'd,
'Twill be so oily, and so sleek
When I have lain in it a week!
You'll find it well prepar'd to take
The figure of toopee or snake.
Thus drest alike from top to toe,
That which is which, 'tis hard to know.
When first in public we appear,
I'll lead the van, keep you the rear.
Be careful, as you walk behind,
Use all the talents of your mind.
Be studious well to imitate
My portly motion, mien and gait.
Mark my address, and learn my style,
When to look scornful, when to smile,
Nor sputter out your oaths so fast,
But keep your swearing to the last.
Then at our leisure we'll be witty,
And in the streets divert the city
The ladies from the windows gaping:
The children all our motions aping.
Your conversation to refine,
I'll take you to some friends of mine;
Choice spirits, who employ their parts,
To mend the world by useful arts.
Some cleansing hollow tubes, to spy
Direct the Zenith of the sky;
Some have the city in their care,
From noxious steams to purge the air;
Some teach us in these dang'rous days,
How to walk upright in our ways;
Some whose reforming hands engage,
To lash the lewdness of the age;
Some for the public service go,
Perpetual envoys to and fro;
Whose able heads support the weight,
Of twenty ministers of state.

59

We scorn, for want of talk, to jabber
Of parties o'er our Bonny-Clabber.
Nor are we studious to enquire,
Who votes for manners, who for hire.
Our care is to improve the mind,
With what concerns all human kind,
The various scenes of mortal life,
Who beats her husband, who his wife;
Or how the bully at a stroke
Knockt down the boy, the lanthorn broke;
One tells the rise of cheese, and oat-meal,
Another when he got a hot meal;
One gives advice in proverbs old,
Instructs us how to tame a scold;
Or how by almanacs 'tis clear,
That herrings will be cheap this year.
   T. Dear Mullinix, I now lament
My precious time, so long mis-spent,
By nature meant for nobler ends,
O, introduce me to your friends!
For whom, by birth, I was design'd,
'Till politics debas'd my mind.
I give my self entire to you,
God damn the Whigs and Tories too.

TOM MULLINEX AND DICK

Tom and Dick had equal fame,
  And both had equal knowledge;
Tom could write and spell his name,
  But Dick had seen a college.

Dick a coxcomb, Tom was mad,
  And both alike diverting,
Tom was held the merrier lad,
  But Dick the best at farting.

Dick would cock his nose in scorn,
  But Tom was kind and loving;
Tom a foot-boy bred and born,
  But Dick was from an oven.

Dick could neatly dance a jig,
  But Tom was best at Borees;
Tom would pray for ev'ry Whig,
  And Dick curse all the Tories.

Dick would make a woeful noise,
  And scold at an election;
Tom huzza'd the black-guard boys,
  And held them in subjection.

Tom could move with lordly grace,
  Dick nimbly skip the gutter;
Tom could talk with solemn face,
  But Dick could better sputter.

Dick was come to high renown
  Since he commenc'd physician;
Tom was held by all the town
  The deeper politician.

Tom had the genteeler swing,
  His hat could nicely put on;
Dick knew better how to swing
  His cane upon a button.

Dick for repartee was fit,
  And Tom for deep discerning;
Dick was thought the brighter wit,
  But Tom had better learning.

Dick with zealous No's and Ay's,
  Could roar as loud as Stentor,
In the House 'tis all he says;
  But Tom is eloquenter.

DICK, A MAGGOT

As when rooting in a bin,
All powder'd o'er from tail to chin;
A lively maggot sallies out,
You know him by his hazel snout:
So, when the grandson of his grandsire,
Forth issues wriggling Dick Drawcensir,
With powder'd rump, and back and side,
You cannot blanch his tawny hide;
For 'tis beyond the pow'r of meal,
The gipsy visage to conceal:
For, as he shakes his wainscot chops,
Down ev'ry mealy atom drops
And leaves the Tartar phiz, in show
Like a fresh turd just dropt on snow.

A PASTORAL DIALOGUE between Dermot and Sheelah

A nymph and swain, Sheelah and Dermot hight,
Who wont to weed the court of Gosford Knight,
While each with stubbed knife remov'd the roots
That rais'd between the stones their daily shoots;

As at their work they sate in counterview,
With mutual beauty smit, their passion grew.
Sing heavenly Muse in sweetly flowing strain,
The soft endearments of the nymph and swain.

DERMOT
  My love to Sheelah is more firmly fixt
Than strongest weeds that grow these stones betwixt:
My spud these nettles from the stone can part,
No knife so keen to weed thee from my heart.

SHEELAH
  My love for gentle Dermot faster grows
Than yon tall dock that rises to thy nose.
Cut down the dock, 'twill sprout again: but O!
Love rooted out, again will never grow.

DERMOT
  No more that briar thy tender leg shall rake:
(I spare the thistle for Sir Arthur's sake).
Sharp are the stones, take thou this rushy mat;
The hardest bum will bruise with sitting squat.

SHEELAH
  Thy breeches torn behind, stand gaping wide;
This petticoat shall save thy dear back-side;
Nor need I blush, although you feel it wet;
Dermot, I vow, 'tis nothing else but sweat.

DERMOT
  At an old stubborn root I chanc'd to tug,
When the Dean threw me this tobacco-plug:
A longer half-p'orth never did I see;
This, dearest Sheelah, thou shalt share with me.

SHEELAH
  In at the pantry-door this morn I slipt,
And from the shelf a charming crust I whipt:
Dennis was out, and I got hither safe;
And thou, my dear, shalt have the bigger half.

DERMOT
  When you saw Tady at long-bullets play,
You sat and lous'd him all the sun-shine day.
How could you, Sheelah, listen to his tales,
Or crack such lice as his betwixt your nails?

SHEELAH
  When you with Oonah stood behind a ditch,
I peept, and saw you kiss the dirty bitch.
Dermot, how could you touch those nasty sluts!
I almost wisht this spud were in your guts.

DERMOT
  If Oonah once I kiss'd, forbear to chide:
Her aunt's my gossip by my father's side:
But, if I ever touch her lips again,
May I be doom'd for life to weed in rain.

SHEELAH
  Dermot, I swear, tho' Tady's locks could hold
Ten thousand lice, and ev'ry louse was gold,
Him on my lap you never more should see;
Or may I loose my weeding-knife—and thee.

DERMOT
  O, could I earn for thee, my lovely lass,
A pair of brogues to bear thee dry to mass!
But see, where Norah with the Sowins comes—
Then let us rise, and rest our weary bums.

ON BURNING A DULL POEM

An ass's hoof alone can hold
That pois'nous juice which kills by cold.
Methought, when I this poem read,
No vessel but an ass's head,
Such frigid fustian could contain;
I mean the head without the brain.
The cold conceits, the chilling thoughts,
Went down like stupefying draughts:
I found my head began to swim,
A numbness crept through ev'ry limb:

In haste, with imprecautions dire,
I threw the volume in the fire:
When, who could think, tho' cold as ice,
It burnt to ashes in a trice.

How could I more enhance its fame?
Though born in snow, it died in flame.

TRAULUS
The first Part: in a Dialogue between Tom and Robin

TOM
Say, Robin, what can Traulus mean
By bell'wing thus against the Dean?
Why does he call him paltry scribbler,
Papist, and Jacobite, and lib'ller?
Yet cannot prove a single fact.

ROBIN
Forgive him, Tom, his head is crackt.

TOM
What mischief can the Dean have done him,
That Traulus calls for vengeance on him?
Why must he sputter, spaul and slaver it
In vain, against the people's fav'rite?
Revile that nation-saving paper,
Which gave the Dean the name of Draper?

ROBIN
Why Tom, I think the case is plain,
Party and spleen have turn'd his brain.

TOM
Such friendship never man profest,
The Dean was never so carest:

For Traulus long his rancour nurst,
Till, God knows why, at last it burst.
That clumsy outside of a porter,
How could it thus conceal a courtier?

ROBIN
I own, appearances are bad;
But still insist the man is mad.

TOM
  Yet many a wretch in Bedlam, knows,
How to distinguish friends from foes;
And tho' perhaps among the rout,
He wildly flings his filth about,
He still has gratitude and sap'ence,
To spare the folks that gave him ha'pence
Nor, in their eyes at random pisses,
But turns aside like mad Ulysses:
While Traulus all his ordure scatters,
To foul the man he chiefly flatters.
Whence come these inconsistent fits?

ROBIN
Why Tom, the man has lost his wits!

TOM
  Agreed. And yet, when Towzer snaps
At people's heels with frothy chaps;
Hangs down his head, and drops his tail,
To say he's mad will not avail:
The neighbours all cry, *Shoot him dead,*
Hang, drown, or knock him on the head.
So, Traulus when he first harangu'd,
I wonder why he was not hang'd:
For of the two, without dispute,
Towzer's the less offensive brute.

ROBIN

Tom, you mistake the matter quite;
Your barking curs will seldom bite:
And, though you hear him stut-tut-tut-ter,
He barks as fast as he can utter.
He prates in spite of all impediment
While none believes that what he said he meant:
Puts in his finger and his thumb,
To grope for words, and out they come.
He calls you rogue; there's nothing in it,
He fawns upon you in a minute.
Begs leave to rail, but damn his blood,
He only meant it for your good.
His friendship was exactly tim'd,
He shot before your foes were prim'd:
By this contrivance Mr Dean
By God I'll bring you off as clean.—
Then let him use you e'er so rough,
'Twas all for love, and that's enough.
For let him sputter thro' a session,
It never makes the least impression.
What e'er he speaks for madness goes,
With no effect on friends or foes.

TOM

The scrubbest cur in all the pack
Can set the mastiffs on your back.
I own, his madness is a jest,
If that were all. But he's possess't:
Incarnate with a thousand imps,
To work whose ends, his madness pimps.
Who o'er each string and wire preside,
Fill ev'ry pipe, each motion guide.
Directing ev'ry vice we find
In scripture, to the Dev'l assign'd:
Sent from the dark infernal region
In him they lodge, and make him *Legion*.

Of *Brethren* he's *a false accuser*,
A sland'rer, traitor and seducer;
A fawning, base, trepanning liar,
The marks peculiar of his sire.
  Or, grant him but a drone at best:
A drone can raise a hornet's nest:
The Dean hath felt their stings before;
And, must their malice ne'er give o'er?
Still swarm and buzz about his nose?
But Ireland's friends ne'er wanted foes.
A patriot is a dang'rous post
When wanted by his country most;
Perversely comes in evil times,
Where virtues are imputed crimes,
His guilt is clear the proofs are pregnant,
A traitor to the vices regnant.
  What spirit since the world began,
Could *always* bear to *strive with man?*
Which God pronounc'd he never wou'd,
And soon convinc'd them by a Floud.
Yet still the Dean on freedom raves,
His spirit always strives with slaves.
'Tis time at last to spare his ink,
And let them rot, or hang, or sink.

AN EXCELLENT NEW BALLAD:
Or, The True English Dean to be Hang'd for a Rape

I.
Our brethren of England who love us so dear,
And in all they do for us so kindly do mean,
A blessing upon them, have sent us this year,
For the good of our Church a true English Dean.
  A holier priest ne'er was wrapt up in crape,
The worst you can say, he committed a rape.

II.

  In his journey to Dublin, he lighted at Chester,
  And there he grew fond of another man's wife,
  Burst into her chamber, and wou'd have carest her,
  But she valu'd her honour much more than her life.
    She bustled and struggled, and made her escape,
  To a room full of guests for fear of a rape.

III.

  The Dean he pursu'd to recover his game,
  And now to attack her again he prepares,
  But the company stood in defence of the dame,
  They cudgell'd, and cuft him, and kickt him down stairs.
    His Deanship was now in a damnable scrape,
  And this was no time for committing a rape.

IV.

  To Dublin he comes, to the Bagnio he goes,
  And orders the landlord to bring him a whore;
  No scruple came on him his gown to expose,
  'Twas what all his life he had practis'd before.
    He had made himself drunk with the juice of the grape,
  And got a good clap, but committed no rape.

V.

  The Dean, and his landlord, a jolly comrade,
  Resolv'd for a fortnight to swim in delight,
  For why, they had both been brought up to the trade
  Of drinking all day, and of whoring all night.
    His landlord was ready his Deanship to ape
  In ev'ry debauch, but committing a rape.

VI.

  This Protestant zealot, this English divine
  In Church and in state was of principles sound,
  Was truer than Steele to the Hanover line,
  And griev'd that a Tory should live above ground.

Shall a subject so loyal be hang'd by the nape,
For no other crime but committing a rape.

VII.

By old Popish canons, as wise men have penn'd 'em,
Each priest had a concubine, *jure Ecclesiae*;
Who'd be Dean of Ferns without a *Commendam*?
And precedents we can produce, if it please ye,
    Then, why should the Dean, when whores are so cheap,
Be put to the peril, and toil of a rape?

VIII.

If fortune should please but to take such a crotchet,
(To thee I apply great Smedley's successor)
To give thee lawn-sleeves a Mitre and Rochet,
Whom would'st thou resemble? I leave thee a guesser;
    But I only behold thee in Atherton's shape,
For sodomy hang'd, as thou for a rape.

IX.

Ah! dost thou not envy the brave Colonel Chartres,
Condemn'd for thy crime, at three score and ten?
To hang him all England would lend him their garters;
Yet he lives, and is ready to ravish agen,
    Then throttle thy self with an ell of strong tape,
For thou hast not a groat to atone for a rape.

X.

The Dean he was vext that his whores were so willing,
He long'd for a girl that would struggle and squall,
He ravish'd her fairly, and sav'd a good shilling;
But, here was to pay the Devil and all.
    His trouble and sorrows now come in a heap,
And hang'd he must be for committing a rape.

XI.

If maidens are ravish't, it is their own choice,
Why are they so wilful to struggle with men?

If they would but lie quiet, and stifle their voice,
No Devil nor Dean could ravish 'em then,
    Nor would there be need of a strong hempen cape,
Tied round the Dean's neck, for committing a rape.

XII.
    Our Church and our state dear England maintains,
For which all true Protestant hearts should be glad;
She sends us our bishops and judges and deans,
And better would give us, if better she had;
    But, Lord how the rabble will stare and will gape,
When the good English Dean is hang'd up for a rape.

THE CHARACTER OF SIR ROBERT WALPOLE
(in imitation of a lampoon on Cardinal Fleury)

With favour & fortune fastidiously blest
he's loud in his laugh & he's coarse in his jest
of favour & fortune unmerited vain
a sharper in trifles a dupe in the main
achieving of nothing still promising wonders
by dint of experience improving in blunders
oppressing true merit exalting the base
and selling his country to purchase his peace
a jobber of stocks by retailing false news
a prater at Court in the style of the stews
of virtue & worth by profession a giber
of juries & senates the bully & briber
Tho I name not the wretch you know who I mean
T'is the cur dog of Britain & spaniel of Spain.

VERSES ON THE DEATH OF DR SWIFT, D.S.P.D.
occasioned by reading a Maxim in Rochefoucauld

As Rochefoucauld his Maxim drew
From nature, I believe 'em true:
They argue no corrupted mind
In him; the fault is in mankind.

   This Maxim more than all the rest
Is thought too base for human breast;
'In all distresses of our friends
We first consult our private ends,
While nature kindly bent to ease us,
Points out some circumstance to please us.'

   If this perhaps your patience move
Let reason and experience prove.

   We all behold with envious eyes,
Our *equal* rais'd above our *size*;
Who would not at a crowded show,
Stand high himself, keep others low?
I love my friend as well as you,
But would not have him stop my view;
Then let me have the higher post;
I ask but for an inch at most.

   If in a battle you should find,
One, whom you love of all mankind,
Had some heroic action done,
A champion kill'd, or trophy won;
Rather than thus be over-topt,
Would you not wish his laurels cropt?

   Dear honest Ned is in the gout,
Lies rackt with pain, and you without:
How patiently you hear him groan!
How glad the case is not your own!

What poet would not grieve to see,
His brethren write as well as he?
But rather than they should excel,
He'd wish his rivals all in hell.

Her end when Emulation misses,
She turns to envy, stings and hisses:
The strongest friendship yields to pride,
Unless the odds be on our side.

Vain human kind! Fantastic race!
Thy various follies, who can trace?
Self-love, ambition, envy, pride,
Their empire in our hearts divide:
Give others riches, power, and station,
'Tis all on me an usurpation.
I have no title to aspire;
Yet, when you sink, I seem the higher.
In Pope, I cannot read a line,
But with a sigh, I wish it mine:
When he can in one couplet fix
More sense than I can do in six:
It gives me such a jealous fit,
I cry, Pox take him, and his wit.

Why must I be outdone by Gay,
In my own hum'rous biting way?

Arbuthnot is no more my friend,
Who dares to irony pretend;
Which I was born to introduce,
Refin'd it first, and show'd its use.

St John, as well as Pultney knows,
That I had some repute for prose;
And till they drove me out of date,
Could maul a minister of state:

If they have mortified my pride,
And made me throw my pen aside;
If with such talents Heav'n hath blest 'em
Have I not reason to detest 'em?

To all my foes, dear Fortune, send
Thy gifts, but never to my friend:
I tamely can endure the first,
But, this with envy makes me burst.

Thus much may serve by way of proem,
Proceed we therefore to our poem.

The time is not remote, when I
Must by the course of nature die:
When I foresee my special friends,
Will try to find their private ends:
Tho' it is hardly understood,
Which way my death can do them good;
Yet, thus methinks, I hear 'em speak;
See, how the Dean begins to break:
Poor gentleman, he droops apace,
You plainly find it in his face:
That old vertigo in his head,
Will never leave him, till he's dead:
Besides, his memory decays,
He recollects not what he says;
He cannot call his friends to mind;
Forgets the place where last he din'd:
Plies you with stories o'er and o'er,
He told them fifty times before.
How does he fancy we can sit,
To hear his out-of-fashion'd wit?
But he takes up with younger folks,
Who for his wine will bear his jokes:
Faith, he must make his stories shorter,
Or change his comrades once a quarter:

In half the time, he talks them round;
There must another set be found.

For poetry, he's past his prime,
He takes an hour to find a rhyme:
His fire is out, his wit decay'd,
His fancy sunk, his Muse a jade.
I'd have him throw away his pen;
But there's no talking to some men.

And, then their tenderness appears,
By adding largely to my years:
'He's older than he would be reckon'd,
And well remembers Charles the Second.

'He hardly drinks a pint of wine;
And that, I doubt, is no good sign.
His stomach too begins to fail:
Last year we thought him strong and hale;
But now, he's quite another thing;
I wish he may hold out till spring.'

Then hug themselves, and reason thus;
'It is not yet so bad with us.'

In such a case they talk in tropes,
And, by their fears express their hopes:
Some great misfortune to portend,
No enemy can match a friend;
With all the kindness they profess,
The merit of a lucky guess,
(When daily howd'y's come of course,
And servants answer; *Worse and worse*)
Wou'd please 'em better than to tell,
That, God be prais'd, the Dean is well.
Then he who prophesied the best,
Approves his foresight to the rest:

'You know, I always fear'd the worst,
And often told you so at first':
He'd rather choose that I should die,
Than his prediction prove a lie.
Not one foretells I shall recover;
But, all agree, to give me over.

Yet should some neighbour feel a pain,
Just in the parts, where I complain;
How many a message would he send?
What hearty prayers that I should mend?
Enquire what regimen I kept;
What gave me ease, and how I slept?
And more lament, when I was dead,
Than all the sniv'llers round my bed.

My good companions, never fear,
For though you may mistake a year;
Though your prognostics run too fast,
They must be verified at last.

'Behold the fatal day arrive!
How is the Dean? He's just alive.
Now the departing prayer is read:
He hardly breathes. The Dean is dead.
Before the passing-bell begun,
The news thro' half the town has run.
O, may we all for death prepare!
What has he left? And who's his heir?
I know no more than what the news is,
'Tis all bequeathed to public uses.
To public use! A perfect whim!
What had the public done for him!
Mere envy, avarice and pride!
He gave it all:—But first he died.
And had the Dean, in all the nation,
No worthy friend, no poor relation?

So ready to do strangers good,
Forgetting his own flesh and blood?'

Now Grub-Street wits are all employ'd;
With elegies, the town is cloy'd:
Some paragraph in ev'ry paper,
To *curse* the *Dean*, or *bless* the *Drapier*.

The doctors tender of their fame,
Wisely on me lay all the blame:
'We must confess his case was nice;
But he would never take advice:
Had he been rul'd, for ought appears,
He might have liv'd these twenty years:
For when we open'd him we found,
That all his vital parts were sound.'

From Dublin soon to London spread,
'Tis told at Court, the Dean is dead.

Kind Lady Suffolk in the spleen,
Runs laughing up to tell the Queen.
The Queen, so gracious, mild and good,
Cries, 'Is he gone? 'Tis time he should.
He's dead you say; why let him rot;
I'm glad the medals were forgot.
I promis'd them, I own; but when?
I only was the Princess then;
But now as Consort of the King,
You know 'tis quite a different thing.'

Now, Chartres at Sir Robert's levee
Tells, with a sneer, the tidings heavy:
'Why, is he dead without his shoes?'
(Cries Bob) 'I'm sorry for the news;
Oh, were the wretch but living still,
And in his place my good friend Will;

Or, had a mitre on his head
Provided Bolingbroke were dead.'

Now Curl his shop from rubbish drains;
Three genuine tomes of Swift's remains.
And then to make them pass the glibber,
Revis'd by Tibbalds, Moore, and Cibber.
He'll treat me as he does my betters.
Publish my will, my life, my letters.
Revive the libels born to die;
Which Pope must bear, as well as I.

Here shift the scene, to represent
How those I love, my death lament.
Poor Pope will grieve a month; and Gay
A week; and Arbuthnot a day.

St John himself will scarce forbear,
To bite his pen, and drop a tear.
The rest will give a shrug and cry
I'm sorry; but we all must die.
Indifference clad in wisdom's guise,
All fortitude of mind supplies:
For how can stony bowels melt,
In those who never pity felt;
When *we* are lash'd, *they* kiss the rod;
Resigning to the will of God.

The fools, my juniors by a year,
Are tortur'd with suspense and fear.
Who wisely thought my age a screen,
When death approach'd, to stand between:
The screen remov'd, their hearts are trembling,
They mourn for me without dissembling.

My female friends, whose tender hearts
Have better learn'd to act their parts,

Receive the news in *doleful dumps*,
'The Dean is dead, (*and what is trumps?*)
Then Lord have mercy on his soul.
(Ladies I'll venture for the Vole.)
Six Deans they say must bear the pall.
(I wish I knew what King to call.)
Madam, your husband will attend
The funeral of so good a friend.
No Madam, 'tis a shocking sight,
And he's engag'd to-morrow night!
My Lady Club wou'd take it ill
If you shou'd fail her at Quadrill.
He lov'd the Dean. (*I lead a heart.*)
But dearest friends, they say, must part.
His time was come, he ran his race;
We hope he's in a better place.'

　　Why do we grieve that friends should die?
No loss more easy to supply.
One year is past; a different scene;
No further mention of the Dean;
Who now, alas, no more is mist,
Than if he never did exist.
Where's now the fav'rite of Apollo?
Departed; *and his works must follow*:
Must undergo the common fate;
His kind of wit is out of date.
Some country squire to Lintot goes,
Enquires for Swift in verse and prose:
Says Lintot, 'I have heard the name:
He died a year ago.' The same.
He searcheth all his shop in vain;
'Sir you may find them in Duck-lane:
I sent them with a load of books,
Last Monday to the pastry-cooks.
To fancy they could live a year!
I find you're but a stranger here.

The Dean was famous in his time;
And had a kind of knack at rhyme:
His way of writing now is past;
The town hath got a better taste:
I keep no antiquated stuff;
But, spick and span I have enough.
Pray, do but give me leave to show 'em;
Here's Colley Cibber's Birth-day Poem.
This Ode you never yet have seen,
By Stephen Duck, upon the Queen.
Then, here's a Letter finely penn'd
Against the Craftsman and his friend;
It clearly shows that all reflection
On ministers, is disaffection.
Next, here's Sir Robert's Vindication,
And Mr Henly's last Oration:
The hawkers have not got 'em yet,
Your Honour please to buy a set?

   'Here's Wolston's Tracts, the twelfth edition;
'Tis read by ev'ry politician:
The country members, when in town,
To all their boroughs send them down:
You never met a thing so smart;
The courtiers have them all by heart:
Those Maids of Honour (who can read)
Are taught to use them for their creed.
The Rev'rend author's good intention,
Hath been rewarded with a pension:
He doth an honour to his gown,
By bravely running priest-craft down:
He shows, as sure as God's in Gloster,
That Jesus was a Grand Imposter:
That all his miracles were cheats,
Perform'd as jugglers do their feats:
The Church had never such a writer:
A shame, he hath not got a mitre!'

Suppose me dead; and then suppose
A club assembled at the Rose;
Where from discourse of this and that,
I grow the subject of their chat:
And, while they toss my name about,
With favour some, and some without;
One quite indiff'rent in the cause,
My character impartial draws:

'The Dean, if we believe report,
Was never ill receiv'd at Court:
As for his works in verse and prose,
I own my self no judge of those:
Nor, can I tell what critics thought 'em;
But, this I know, all people bought 'em;
As with a moral view design'd
To cure the vices of mankind:
His vein, ironically grave,
Expos'd the fool, and lash'd the knave:
To steal a hint was never known,
But what he writ was all his own.

'He never thought an honour done him,
Because a Duke was proud to own him:
Would rather slip aside, and choose
To talk with wits in dirty shoes:
Despis'd the fools with stars and garters,
So often seen caressing Chartres:
He never courted men in station,
Nor persons had in admiration;
Of no man's greatness was afraid,
Because he sought for no man's aid.
Though trusted long in great affairs,
He gave himself no haughty airs:
Without regarding private ends,
Spent all his credit for his friends:
And only chose the wise and good;

No flatt'rers; no allies in blood;
But succour'd virtue in distress,
And seldom fail'd of good success;
As numbers in their hearts must own,
Who, but for him, had been unknown.

'With Princes kept a due decorum,
But never stood in awe before 'em:
And to her Majesty, God bless her,
Would speak as free as to her dresser,
She thought it his peculiar whim,
Nor took it ill as come from him.
He follow'd David's lesson just,
In Princes never put thy trust.
And, would you make him truly sour;
Provoke him with *a slave in Power*:
The Irish Senate, if you nam'd,
With what impatience he declaim'd!
Fair LIBERTY was all his cry;
For her he stood prepar'd to die;
For her he boldly stood alone;
For her he oft expos'd his own.
Two kingdoms, just as faction led,
Had set a price upon his head;
But, not a traitor could be found,
To sell him for six hundred pound.

'Had he but spar'd his tongue and pen,
He might have rose like other men:
But, power was never in his thought;
And, wealth he valu'd not a groat:
Ingratitude he often found,
And pitied those who meant the wound:
But, kept the tenor of his mind,
To merit well of human kind:
Nor made a sacrifice of those
Who still were true, to please his foes.

He labour'd many a fruitless hour
To reconcile his friends in power;
Saw mischief by a faction brewing,
While they pursu'd each other's ruin.
But, finding vain was all his care,
He left the Court in mere despair.

'And, oh! how short are human schemes!
Here ended all our golden dreams.
What St John's skill in state affairs,
What Ormond's valour, Oxford's cares,
To save their sinking country lent,
Was all destroy'd by one event.
Too soon that precious life was ended,
On which alone, our weal depended.
When up a dangerous faction starts,
With wrath and vengeance in their hearts:
By solemn league and cov'nant bound,
To ruin, slaughter and confound;
To turn Religion to a fable,
And make the government a Babel:
Pervert the Law, disgrace the Gown,
Corrupt the Senate, rob the Crown;
To sacrifice old England's glory,
And make her infamous in story.
When such a tempest shook the land,
How could unguarded virtue stand?

'With horror, grief, despair the Dean
Beheld the dire destructive scene:
His friends in exile, or the Tower,
Himself within the frown of power;
Pursu'd by base envenom'd pens,
Far to the land of slaves and fens;
A servile race in folly nurs'd,
Who truckle most, when treated worst.

'By innocence and resolution,
He bore continual persecution;
While numbers to preferment rose;
Whose merits were, to be his foes.
When, *e'en his own familiar friends*
Intent upon their private ends;
Like renegados now he feels,
Against him lifting up their heels.

'The Dean did by his pen defeat
An infamous destructive cheat.
Taught fools their int'rest how to know;
And gave them arms to ward the blow.
Envy hath own'd it was his doing,
To save that helpless land from ruin,
While they who at the steerage stood,
And reapt the profit, sought his blood.

'To save them from their evil fate,
In him was held a crime of state.
A wicked monster on the bench,
Whose fury blood could never quench;
As vile and profligate a villain,
As modern Scroggs, or old Tressilian;
Who long all justice had discarded,
Nor fear'd he GOD, nor man regarded;
Vow'd on the Dean his rage to vent,
And make him of his zeal repent;
But Heav'n his innocence defends,
The grateful people stand his friends:
Not strains of law, nor judge's frown,
Nor topics brought to please the Crown,
Nor witness hir'd, nor jury pick'd,
Prevail to bring him in convict.

'In exile with a steady heart,
He spent his life's declining part;

84

Where, folly, pride and faction sway,
Remote from St John, Pope and Gay.

   'His friendship there to few confin'd,
Were always of the middling kind:
No fools of rank, a mongrel breed,
Who fain would pass for lords indeed:
Where titles give no right or power,
And peerage is a wither'd flower,
He would have held it a disgrace,
If such a wretch had known his face.
On rural squires, that kingdom's bane,
He vented oft his wrath in vain:
Biennial squires, to market brought;
Who sell their souls and votes for naught;
The nation stript go joyful back,
To rob the Church, their tenants rack,
Go snacks with thieves and rapparees,
And, keep the peace, to pick up fees:
In every job to have a share,
A jail or barrack to repair;
And turn the tax for public roads
Commodious to their own abodes.

   'Perhaps I may allow, the Dean
Had too much satire in his vein;
And seem'd determin'd not to starve it,
Because no age could more deserve it.
Yet, malice never was his aim;
He lash'd the vice but spar'd the name.
No individual could resent
Where thousands equally were meant.
His satire points at no defect,
But what all mortals may correct;
For he abhorr'd that senseless tribe,
Who call it humour when they gibe:
He spar'd a hump or crooked nose,

Whose owners set not up for beaux.
True genuine dullness mov'd his pity,
Unless it offer'd to be witty.
Those, who their ignorance confess'd,
He ne'er offended with a jest;
But laugh'd to hear an idiot quote,
A verse from Horace, learn'd by rote.

'He knew an hundred pleasant stories,
With all the turns of Whigs and Tories:
Was cheerful to his dying day,
And friends would let him have his way.

'He gave the little wealth he had,
To build a house for fools and mad:
And show'd by one satiric touch,
No nation wanted it so much:
That kingdom he hath left his debtor,
I wish it soon may have a better.'

HELTER SKELTER, or, The Hue and Cry after the
Attornies, going to ride the Circuit

Now the active young attornies
Briskly travel on their journies,
Looking big as any giants,
On the horses of their clients;
Like so many little Mars's,
With their tilters at their arses,
Brazen hilted lately burnish'd,
And with harness-buckles furnish'd;
And with whips and spurs so neat,
And with jockey-coats complete;
And with boots so very grazy
And with saddles eke so easy
And with bridles fine and gay,

Bridles borrow'd for a day,
Bridles destin'd far to roam,
Ah! never to return home;
And the hats so very big, sir;
And with powder'd caps and wigs, sir;
And with ruffles to be shown,
Cambric ruffles not their own;
And with Holland shirts so white,
Shirts becoming to the sight,
Shirts be wrought with different letters,
As belonging to their betters:
With their pretty tinsel'd boxes,
Gotten from their dainty doxies,
And with rings so very trim,
Lately taken out of Lim—
And with very little pence,
And as very little sense:
With some law but little justice,
Having stolen from mine hostess,
From the barber and the cutler,
Like the soldier from the sutler;
From the vintner and the tailor,
Like the felon from the jailer,
Into this and t'other county,
Living on the public bounty;
Thorough town and thorough village,
All to plunder, all to pillage;
Thorough mountains thorough valleys;
Thorough stinking lanes and alleys;
Some to cuckold farmers' spouses,
And make merry in their houses;
Some to tumble country-wenches
On their rushy beds and benches,
And, if they begin a fray,
Draw their swords and run away:
All to murder equity,
And to take a double fee;

Till the people all are quiet
And forget to broil and riot,
Low in pocket, cow'd in courage,
Safely glad to sup their porridge,
And vacation's over—then
Hey for Dublin town agen!

THE PLACE OF THE DAMN'D

All folks who pretend to religion and grace,
Allow there's a Hell, but dispute of the place;
But if Hell may by logical rules be defin'd,
The place of the damn'd,—I will tell you my mind.
  Wherever the damn'd do chiefly abound,
Most certainly there is Hell to be found,
Damn'd Poets, damn'd critics, damn'd block-heads, damn'd knaves,
Damn'd senators brib'd, damn'd prostitute slaves;
Damn'd lawyers and judges, damn'd lords and damn'd squires,
Damn'd spies and informers, damn'd friends and damn'd liars;
Damn'd villains, corrupted in every station,
Damn'd time-serving priests all over the nation;
And into the bargain, I'll readily give you,
Damn'd ignorant prelates, and councillors privy.
Then let us no longer by parsons be flamm'd,
For we know by these marks, the place of the damn'd;
And Hell to be sure is at Paris or Rome,
How happy for us, that it is not at home.

*EPIGRAM on seeing a worthy Prelate go out of Church in the Time
of Divine Service, to wait on his Grace the Duke of Dorset*

Lord Pam in the Church (could you think it) kneel'd down,
When told the Lieutenant was just come to town,
His station despising, unaw'd by the place,
He flies from his God, to attend on his Grace:

To the Court it was fitter to pay his devotion,
Since God had no hand in his Lordship's promotion.

'DEAF, GIDDY, HELPLESS. . .'

Deaf, giddy, helpless, left alone,
To all my friends a burthen grown,
No more I hear my church's bell,
Than if it rang out for my knell:
At thunder now no more I start,
Than at the rumbling of a cart:
Nay, what's incredible, alack!
I hardly hear a woman's clack.

'EVER EATING, NEVER CLOYING . . .'

Ever eating, never cloying,
All devouring, all destroying,
Never finding full repast,
Till I eat the world at last.

AN EPIGRAM ON SCOLDING

Great folks are of a finer mould;
Lord! how politely they can scold;
While a coarse English tongue will itch,
For whore and rogue; and dog and bitch.

VERSES made for Women who cry Apples, &c.

APPLES
Come buy my fine wares,
Plums, apples and pears,
A hundred a penny,
In conscience too many,
Come, will you have any;
My children are seven,
I wish them in Heaven,
My husband's a sot,
With his pipe and his pot,
Not a farthing will gain 'em,
And I must maintain 'em.

ASPARAGUS
Ripe 'sparagrass,
  Fit for lad or lass,
To make their water pass:
  O, 'tis pretty picking
  With a tender chicken.

ONIONS
Come, follow me by the smell,
Here's delicate onions to sell,
I promise to use you well.
They make the blood warmer,
You'll feed like a farmer:
For this is ev'ry cook's opinion,
No sav'ry dish without an onion;
But lest your kissing should be spoil'd,
Your onions must be th'roughly boil'd;
  Or else you may spare
  Your mistress a share,
The secret will never be known;
  She cannot discover
  The breath of her lover,
But think it as sweet as her own.

OYSTERS

Charming oysters I cry,
My masters come buy,
So plump and so fresh,
So sweet is their flesh,
No Colchester oyster,
Is sweeter and moister,
Your stomach they settle,
And rouse up your mettle,
They'll make you a dad
Of a lass or a lad;
And, madam your wife
They'll please to the life;
Be she barren, be she old,
Be she slut, or be she scold,
Eat my oysters, and lie near her,
She'll be fruitful, never fear her.

HERRINGS

Be not sparing,
Leave off swearing
Buy my herring
Fresh from Malahide,
Better ne'er was tried.
Come eat 'em with pure fresh butter and mustard,
Their bellies are soft, and as white as a custard,
Come, six-pence a dozen to get me some bread,
Or, like my own herrings, I soon shall be dead.

ORANGES

Come, buy my fine oranges, sauce for your veal,
And charming when squeez'd in a pot of brown ale.
Well roasted, with sugar and wine in a cup,
They'll make a sweet bishop when gentlefolks sup.